Mortgages Made Simple

Everything You Need To Know About Mortgages

Barry Mitchell

An easy to understand explanation of the world of mortgages

Copyright © 2015 Barry Mitchell
All rights reserved.
ISBN-10: 1508841780
ISBN-13: 978-1508841784

DEDICATION

This book is dedicated to my parents who taught and loved by example and who instilled in me the values and work ethic that has brought me to this point in my life and will continue to do so until the end of my days.

It is dedicated to my wife who has loved me and supported me and has been with me all the way, unwavering through both the good times and the bad. I haven't always made it easy for her.

It is dedicated to my three sons who have experience, a vitality and a zest for life. Their love, outlook, support, drive and youth has provided me with alternative perspectives that makes me and my world a better place because they are inextricably entwined within it.

It is dedicated to my grandson and future grandchildren yet to arrive who are my future and make it all worthwhile.

It is dedicated to my teachers and mentors who are always there to show me the way. They give so much and expect nothing in return.

Mortgages Made Simple

CONTENTS

	Foreword	i
	Introduction	ii
1	**Mortgage Fundamentals**	Pg 1
	• Interest Only Mortgages	
	• Capital & Interest Mortgages (Repayment)	
	• Loan To Value (LTV)	
2	**Explaining Some Of The Jargon**	Pg 11
	• Bank Base Rate	
	• SVR – Standard Variable Rate	
	• Tracker Mortgages	
	• LIBOR	
3	**Mortgage Incentives**	Pg 15
	• Fixed Rate	
	• Discount Rate	
	• Capped Rate	
	• Capped & Collared	
	• Cash Back	
	• Early Repayment Charge (ERC)	
	• Portability	
	• Mortgage Insurance Premium (MIP)	
4	**Flexible Mortgage**	Pg 37
	• Offset Mortgages	
	• Cash Account Mortgages	
5	**Off On A Slight Tangent & Amusing Anecdotes**	Pg 61
	• 130% Rule	
6	**Capital Raising, Releasing Equity and Debt Consolidation**	Pg 69
7	**Equity Release/Lifetime Mortgages and Home Reversion**	Pg 71
8	**Self-Build Mortgages**	Pg 74
9	**Bridging Loans**	Pg 76
10	**Glossary of Terms & Jargon Buster**	Pg 81

Foreword

I purchased my first house at the age of 22 and remember thinking what nice people they were at the building society to agree to let me borrow all that money. I was so naïve and so unprepared for the responsibility of a mortgage but we all were, right? And that is partly the inspiration for this book

After I received my first annual statement, I had to phone the building society to inform them of their error. I can't remember the figures now but I knew that in the course of the year, I had paid this much and yet my balance had only been reduced by a fraction of that amount. The very pleasant person on the other end of the phone explained why there was no error and I remember not understanding a word of the explanation. I just accepted they were right, I was wrong and I just continued to pay my mortgage. Why is it that perfectly nice people, born and brought up in this country (or not as the case might be), who speak perfectly good English in their everyday lives, walk through the doors of that hallowed institution called a bank or a building society and then seem incapable of speaking a language that you and I understand?

This book is for those people who are contemplating their first mortgage, those people who already have a mortgage or perhaps have had several mortgages and never really understood them and for those who are either in the mortgage industry or about to embark on a career within the industry.

Barry Mitchell

INTRODUCTION

Over a period of approximately eight years (2000 – 2008) I presented to well in excess of 40,000 people, all over the UK, the Irish Republic and parts of Spain, providing knowledge, insights and education on how to best invest in property, how to structure the finance and then to arrange the finance. I was even able to demonstrate how, in the right (and legal) circumstances, rather than pay for a property, one could effectively be paid for the privilege of buying a property. I used to ask the question:

"If you could buy a property for nothing or, better still, be paid for the privilege of buying a property, how many would you have?"

Given such powerful knowledge and with all the information I provided, it was a great surprise to me to learn that, consistently, the section that most impressed the most people was my presentation on Understanding Mortgages.

To this day, I cannot get over the amount of people who approached me and said things like 'they have had several mortgages over many years and they never really understood them until they heard my presentation'. The other thing that I was constantly and forever being told was that this sort of thing should be taught in schools and colleges and some people were so animated it sometimes felt they were having a go at me for not offering this to schools

I have tried to avoid jargon as much as possible and have explained it where it is unavoidable. I do hope you get out of this what thousands of people before you have clearly appreciated.

Please note that whilst I hold appropriate qualifications to perform as a mortgage adviser, I choose to no longer be authorised by the appropriate regulatory authority and am not authorised to provide financial advice. This book, therefore, is for educational and informational purposes only and if you do require advice, please contact an appropriately qualified and authorised adviser.

So, how did I get involved in mortgages in the first place? I used to have my own specialist business lining tanks, reservoirs, lakes and lagoons, as well as specialist flat roofing applications, which I ran for approximately fifteen years. I built that business from scratch and with no money to get it started. I loved that business. It was a very successful business but it suffered indirectly because of the stupidity of the banks during the recession of the 1990's.

We all know that in times of recession, the building industry is the first and worse to suffer and I was considered (by the bank) to be working on the periphery of the building industry. They took a blanket decision to call in loans to businesses in the construction industry, including my loan that they asked me to reduce, not clear. They did not bother to look at me or my business. They ignored the fact that my business had no debt whatsoever other than scheduled debt. They ignored the fact that I never, ever missed a payment, that I had enough cash in the bank to keep me fluid for at least three months and that I had both ongoing contracts and contracts in the pipeline, some of which I would have won and some I would not. Not bad for a small company trading through a recession! I knew that if I would pay the money they demanded, that would seriously jeopardise my business. I also asked myself how much work do I have to do in order to earn the sort of money they were demanding and over what period of time? Well, I could write a book on this episode of my life but suffice it to say, the following day after my conversation with the manager, with whom I got on extremely well (that was still in the days when they had bank managers), I went to the bank, withdrew all my money and closed the business there and then. The bank ended up losing approximately £42,000 because of their stupidity and I came out of it unscathed and unemployed.

For something like six months, I was a bit like the rabbit in the headlights and had no idea what I was going to do or how I intended to earn a livelihood.

Fortunately, as luck would have it, I had a chance meeting with someone who was to become a great colleague of mine, who was telling me the extent to which the banks and building societies collectively cheated us and robbed us. The conversation was essentially in two halves joined by a single, powerful, statement that I have never forgotten. The first half, as I said, was about how badly the banks treated us and the second half was what we could do about it. And the statement that joined the two halves? He said:

"The banks and building societies are too big, too powerful and too well established to take on and fight; you cannot win. But what you can do is learn and understand the system and use that for the benefit of your clients rather than the benefit of the banks."

Wow! What a powerful statement. I thought to myself 'I can do that. This could be a great business. And it would be so much more secure, as banks will never go bankrupt'! Right?'

Little did I know!

So, I got trained and went out and demonstrated to clients how they could reduce the overall cost of their mortgage, by many thousands of pounds, over the life of the mortgage, by employing techniques that the banks usually did not allow but I could advise how to circumvent that legally and correctly. My clients could (and did) make the savings I promised. I introduced the concept of what was known then as 'Aussie Mortgages' of which, more later.

This powerful niche lasted for about two years. The reality was that I and people like me were helping the financial institutions lose millions of pounds, there was nothing they could about it and they realised this wasn't going away. I think the last straw was when the Bank of Yorkshire was taken over by an Australian bank and the parent company couldn't understand why all mortgages did not offer the facilities that we were recommending. As a damage limitation exercise, many banks started to offer their own products and this became the birth of the Flexible Mortgage.

I continued to offer these products and developed a new niche around the subject of property investments and the strategic financing of such projects.

1 Mortgage Fundamentals

So, what is the origin of the word 'Mortgage'? It is a strange sounding word when you come to think about it, isn't it?

Actually, it comes from two words; the Latin word 'Mors', meaning death, and the French word 'Gagé' meaning pledge. So a mortgage is a death pledge or, to put it another way, a lifetime commitment.

I don't normally go for dictionary definitions, but if I were to choose one it would be:

'A lien upon land or other property as security for the performance of some obligation, to become void on such performance'.

That is to say, the lender retains an interest in your land/property until you repay the debt plus interest and if you don't keep up with your monthly payments, you are likely to lose your land or property. Why they don't just say that, I do not know.

I would like to start by explaining the difference between an 'Interest Only' mortgage and a 'Capital & Interest' mortgage, more commonly referred to as a 'Repayment Mortgage'.

Interest Only Mortgages

An interest only mortgage is exactly what it says. Imagine you borrow £100,000 over, let's say 25 years, on an interest only basis and every month, month in month out, you pay your monthly payments, all you're doing for those 25 years is paying off the interest. At the end of the 25 years, you still owe the original £100,000 you borrowed. Of course that begs the question, if you still owe £100,000, how do you pay that off? Well, under the latest rules and regulations, your lender is required to satisfy itself that you have the financial means to clear the debt when that becomes due. This means that you will require an adequate repayment vehicle such as an endowment policy, pension plan or some other policy that has the ability and capacity to be worth the amount that you originally borrowed, so that you have the ability to clear the debt when it becomes due (in this example, in twenty-five years' time). So an interest only mortgage is one where you are only paying interest and paying nothing to clear the debt.

People often think that an Endowment Mortgage is another name for an Interest Only mortgage. This is not true. In fact, strictly speaking, there is no such thing as an Endowment Mortgage. I have already defined an interest only mortgage and explained the need for a repayment vehicle, whether that be a suitable pension plan, a savings plan or an endowment policy. So, that's it. If you have an Interest Only mortgage and you have set up an Endowment policy as the means with which to clear the mortgage debt at the due date, then you have an Interest Only mortgage and an Endowment Policy as the repayment vehicle, the so-called Endowment Mortgage.

Capital & Interest Mortgage (Repayment)

A Capital and Interest mortgage, more commonly known as a Repayment Mortgage, is one where your monthly payments are repaying both the interest and the amount you originally borrowed. Therefore, whereas with an interest only mortgage the balance always remains the same, it never reduces, with a repayment mortgage the balance is gradually reduced, so that, provided you kept up with your monthly payments, at the end of the life of the mortgage, you would have cleared your debt and you owe nothing.

As an aside, with an Interest Only mortgage, the monthly payment is the same irrespective of how long you set up the mortgage term. In other words, with an Interest Only mortgage, whether it is for 10 years or 25 years or any other figure, the monthly payment remains the same. With a Repayment Mortgage, the longer the term of the mortgage, the lower the monthly payment but (and here's the bit they don't tell you) the higher the overall cost of the mortgage. So, to repeat that, the longer the term of a Repayment Mortgage, the lower the monthly payment but the greater the overall cost of the mortgage.

I remember, on more than one occasion, people saying to me that they do not wish to change lenders as their lender was very good to them and very understanding when they experienced a spell of financial difficulties. They explained how their lender suggested extending the term of their repayment mortgage in order to reduce the monthly payment. They were such nice people. Now, that may or may not have been the best advice in their circumstances but when I explained that of course they were happy to do that because lenders always take a long-term view and by increasing the term of the mortgage, yes, it reduced the monthly payment but, yes, it also increased the overall cost of the mortgage and the lender increased their profitability. Not such nice people now, are they?

Let me state, here and now, loyalty to any bank, building society or any other lender is always loyalty misplaced and I can assure you they have absolutely no loyalty to you.

Going back to the matter in hand, the important thing for you to understand, is that with a Repayment Mortgage, in the first half of the life of the mortgage, you are paying predominantly interest, and only a little bit of your monthly payment goes towards reducing the actual debt. It is only after you reach the half-way point (after 12 years on a 25-year mortgage) that you are paying more and more off the debt and less and less towards the interest, such that, as I have already stated, at the end of the term of the mortgage, you have cleared your debt and you owe nothing.

So obviously, if a Repayment Mortgage is repaying both interest and the debt, and the Interest Only mortgage is only paying interest, then the monthly repayments on the Repayment Mortgage must be higher than the monthly payment on an Interest Only mortgage, where you borrow the same amount. As a rule of thumb, the monthly payment on a 25 year Interest Only mortgage is approximately two thirds of the monthly payment on a Repayment Mortgage, spread over the same term.

Why is this important to understand? Well, historically and statistically, we move home every seven years and we do this three times in our lifetime. Most people take out a twenty-five year mortgage, not just to purchase their first property but for every subsequent property they purchase and, often, also when they re-mortgage to obtain a better rate of interest, to raise capital, etc. So, given what I stated earlier, that in the first half of a Repayment Mortgage most of the payments go towards the interest and very little to reducing the debt, you will discover that despite the monthly payments you have been making (on a repayment basis) you haven't really received a benefit from paying the higher amount (compared with the monthly payment of the Interest Only equivalent) as the outstanding balance has hardly reduced, relatively speaking.

In other words, in this example, you have been paying a higher amount for 21 years and not received the full benefit of paying this higher amount.

This was the argument that was given to justify having an Endowment Policy and, in my opinion, the argument has validity. If you chose to have an Interest Only mortgage and paid the difference between the monthly payments of the two styles of mortgages into an Endowment Policy or a Pension or some other appropriate repayment vehicle, then all of that payment, notwithstanding the possible initial costs of purchasing, setting up and operating the policy, would contribute to the profitability of the policy and you could operate this policy to run alongside all of the mortgages that you were ever destined to take out, right from day one.

Going back to the idea of changing mortgages three times, once every seven years and recognising that for the first half of a Repayment Mortgage, most of the payment goes towards interest and hardly anything towards reducing the debt, and bearing in mind what I have already stated, that you have twenty-one years of paying an excessive amount and not receiving any real benefit from paying this higher amount, I hope you can now understand why I feel that paying this extra amount into an appropriate savings plan makes sense.

As a general rule, therefore, when looking for a mortgage, just do the maths and let that make the decision for you. The main thing is, you are now aware of what it is you should be questioning.

As a risk management strategy, if you do opt for an Interest Only mortgage with an appropriate savings vehicle, when interest rates go down and, therefore, your monthly mortgage payment is correspondingly reduced, you should resolve to pay 90% of that saving as an increased payment into your repayment vehicle, to ensure it performs as required over the term of the policy. Why not 100%? Well, I want you to enjoy the feel-good factor also and it is always nice to know that your monthly expenditure has just gone down.

In my opinion, the concept of an Endowment Policy is sound, especially since they are now more heavily regulated. The reason they gained an unfavourable reputation was that those selling such policies often failed to explain that their value could go down as well as up and there may not be sufficient funds to clear the mortgage debt at the end of the term.

Imagine, the very worse time to receive the devastating news that your policy has insufficient funds to clear your mortgage debt is as you are possibly thinking about retiring and now, at this late stage in your working life, you are going to have to find a substantial lump sum to subsidise your under-performing policy!

When interest rates were high, these policies were usually very profitable. When interest rates were low, they were less profitable and this could result in the situation that I have already described, where you have come to the end of your 25-year interest only mortgage, you now need to pay back the amount you originally borrowed but the policy is not worth as much as you need to pay the sum necessary to clear your mortgage debt. But, of course, when interest rates went down, unless your mortgage was on a fixed rate of interest, your mortgage payment also went down. As suggested earlier, if people had been advised to re-invest say 90% of the savings they made from reduced mortgage payments back into their savings policy, then the extra payments would have offset the reduced profitability of the policy and probably ensured that the policy remained on target to clear the debt at the due date.

I keep referring to Endowment Policies. I have no real preference over any acceptable style of policy, Endowment, Pension, SIPPs (Self-Invested Personal Pension plans) etc., as long as what is chosen has the capability of achieving the reason it was put in place in the first place. I suppose I am being deliberately contentious by focusing more on Endowment policies as that is the product that has come (unfairly, in my opinion) into disrepute. It wasn't the product, is was the people selling them.

Loan To Value (LTV)

Loan to value or LTV is a piece of jargon that is constantly being used.

The Loan to Value is the amount you are borrowing expressed as a percentage of the value of the property. So, if you are borrowing £60,000 on a £100,000 property, then the LTV is 60%. If you are borrowing £90,000 on a £100,000 property, the LTV is 90%. If you are borrowing £337,500 on a £450,000 property, then the LTV is 75%. Lenders' criteria and various incentives are tied in very heavily to the LTV the lenders are prepared to accept.

2 Explaining Some Of The Jargon

I would now like to explain some of the jargon you are going to come across when dealing with mortgages.

Bank Base Rate

The Bank Base Rate (BBR) is the rate of interest set by the Bank of England. It is the rate paid by banks and other financial institutions for its loans from the Bank of England. It is sometimes referred to as the Bank Rate, the Bank of England Rate, the Base Rate or The Bank of England Bank Base Rate. Whatever they call it, it's all the same. The BBR is set and announced by the Bank of England's Monetary Policy Committee every month.

SVR – Standard Variable Rate.

The standard variable rate is an almost arbitrary rate of interest, set by the lenders as the rate they wish to charge for their mortgages. I say more or less arbitrarily, but in reality they are all much of a muchness as they are all in competition with each other. As the name suggests, this standard rate is variable and it can go up or down, usually reflecting changes in the Bank of England's rate of interest.

The problem with the SVR is that if the Bank of England puts its rate up today, then tomorrow you would receive a letter from your lender, saying something like 'Dear customer, we are absolutely delighted, ecstatic and overjoyed to inform you that your monthly payments have gone up. And as from next month your new payment will be..... whatever.'

On the other hand if interest rates came down, then you would not receive a comparable letter. What you would hear or read is a press release. 'We are going to take a view. We will see how the market performs over the next six months, and then we'll decide what we want to do.' And if they did bring the rates down it often wasn't by as much as the decrease set by the Bank of England six months earlier.

Tracker Mortgages

Not surprisingly people would complain. They are very quick to put the prices up. They are very slow to bring the prices down. One of the responses to these complaints was to introduce products that mirrored the level of the Bank of England rate or, in other words, tracked the rate of the Bank of England and these products are known as Tracker Mortgages.

What they did typically, but not exclusively, was agree that whatever the Bank of England Rate is, we will charge 1.75% above that. Although now, because the interest rate is at an all-time low, the banks are charging a lot more than +1.75%, more like +5.75% although special rates, incentives, etc. are often available for the first few months or years of your new mortgage/product.

So, with a Tracker Mortgage, if the Bank of England rate went up today, then your mortgage rate went up today. If the Bank of England rate went down today, your mortgage rate went down today.

So where the interest rate set by the lender is being defined as a percentage above the Bank of England rate, in other words it is tracking the Bank of England rate, then that type of mortgage is known as a 'Tracker Mortgage'. A tracker mortgage is where the interest rate is tracking the Bank of England rate and all in all it was considered a much fairer way of operating.

However, I don't want to give you the impression that some lenders operate a standard variable rate and that some lenders operate a tracker rate as that is not the case. Virtually all lenders have their standard variable rate and many lenders offer a range of products that track the Bank of England rate of interest.

LIBOR

It used to be the case that only those operating in the world of finance and those with commercial mortgages, including Buy-to-Let mortgages, had ever heard of LIBOR. However, with all the news over the last few years, talking about the disgusting behaviour of the banks concerning the fixing of LIBOR rates, the name has become very familiar but still, the majority of people do not know what LIBOR is. L-I-B-O-R, the London Inter Bank Offered Rate is the wholesale rate at which some lenders buy in money in order that they can lend it out again at a profit. In the past, The LIBOR rate was often the same as the Bank of England rate. Every quarter a panel of lenders met, to decide what their LIBOR rate was going to be for the following quarter. And they (should) make their decision based upon how they think the economy is going to go and how the money markets are going to perform.

Okay, that's the boring side, we now go on to the sexy side of mortgages – and, yes, there is a sexy side.

3 Mortgage Incentives

The fact remains, especially in the good times, you will find there are more lenders with more money than there are people to borrow it. So the lenders are usually falling over themselves to give you money. There are all sorts of incentives out there to try and attract your business to them.

I just want to go over some of the incentives they offer so that you understand how they work and understand the advantages and disadvantages of each..

Fixed Rate

The first incentive I am going to talk about is the Fixed Rate mortgage. This is where the lender will effectively say to you 'If you place your business with us, we will fix the rate of interest at whatever level for a period of time.' So they might say 'bring your mortgage to us and we'll fix a rate of 5%, 3% or 1% or whatever it is, for 3 months, 6 months, 9 months, 1 year, 3 years, 10 years or even the life of the mortgage'.

So in other words, if interest rates in the open market go up and up and up and you have a Fixed Rate mortgage, yours stays fixed at the agreed level, for the agreed period of time and there will be no increase in your monthly payments. On the other hand if interest rates go down and down and down, then what started off as a good deal when you took it out, is not such a good deal now because your monthly payment doesn't go down and you're possibly feeling as sick as the proverbial parrot, knowing that others are probably paying less for their mortgage than you are for yours.

Also, it's worth bearing in mind, that if, whilst your rate has been fixed and during the course of your fixed-rate period, interest rates do go up, it can come as an awful shock when you come to the end of the fixed-rate deal, to find one month you are paying a relatively low monthly mortgage payment and then next month, you suddenly jump to a much higher monthly mortgage payment. That can be very painful and is known within the industry as 'Payment Shock'.

The advantage of a fixed rate is that it can be very, very comforting, to be able to perfectly budget for your mortgage payments for a fixed period of time, irrespective of what is going on in the marketplace generally. This is especially true for a first time buyer who is not used to handling a mortgage and equally for an investor or a landlord who is running a business and needs to be able to budget. So there you have the advantages and disadvantages of a Fixed Rate product.

Discount Rate

An alternative to the fixed rate is a discounted rate. This is where the lender is effectively saying 'if you place your business with us, whatever our rate of interest is, we will reduce it with a discount of 1%, 0.5%, 3% or whatever the deal is at the time.'

So if the lender's standard rate is, say, 5% and they are offering a 2% discount for, say, two years, then for the next two years, if their rate stays at 5%, the rate that you would pay is 3% for the next two years. However, if rates increase in general and your lender increases its Standard Variable Rate to, say 6%, then your new rate would be 4% for the remainder of the two-year period. Similarly, if there were a decrease in the rate of interest, say from 5% to 4% then your rate would go down to 2% for the remainder of the two-year period.

In other words, if during the period of the discount, your lender either increases or decreases its Standard Variable Rate, then your rate will 'mirror' the change in the interest rate, and will go up or down by the same amount that your lender puts its rate either up or down.

Clearly, the incentive of a discount does not allow you to budget in the same way as you can with a Fixed Rate product but if interest rates do go up, at least you have the satisfaction of knowing that whatever anybody else is paying, you're paying less.

On the other hand if interest rates did go down, you would enjoy the benefit of that decrease, a benefit you would not enjoy if the rates went down whist you were on a fixed rate.

There is no right or wrong or 'What is best' – it is just a matter of what you feel works best for you in your circumstances and which you prefer. If you feel interest rates are likely to increase over the next two – five years, it might make sense to go for a fixed rate. If you think there is a possibility that interest rates could go down over the next two – five years, then you might feel a discounted rate would be more prudent. If you're just not sure, listen to well-meaning family and friends by all means, but do take advice from a whole-of-market mortgage adviser. Please do not go to a bank or a building society as they are a business and, like any other business, they have sales targets to achieve and are motivated to make a sale. Furthermore, they are only able to provide advice around the mortgage products that that bank or building society offers and will not look at the whole of market to determine what the best product is for you in your circumstances.

Capped Rate

A Capped Rate is, if you like, a cross between a Fixed Rate and being on the Standard Variable Rate. It is a cap or a ceiling above which the interest rate cannot go for a period of time.

If interest rates increase in general whilst you are on a Capped Rate, then the increase that you may suffer cannot go above the Cap for the period of that deal. So, in that respect it is behaving a bit like a Fixed Rate product. However, if interest rates in general go down, then yours would go down also and you would be on the Standard Variable Rate.

So, whilst you cannot budget in quite the same way as you can with a Fixed Rate product, at least you know there is point above which it cannot go, for a period of time, but you can enjoy a reduction if rates do go down, something you cannot do if you're on a Fixed Rate.

Capped and Collared

I have included this for the sake of being thorough but a Collar is not an incentive, more a restriction. You tend to see Capped and Collared incentives when interest rates are generally very high or, indeed, when they are very low. That is why, after 2008, some Collar mortgages were introduced after the Bank of England reduced its Base Rate to 0.5%. If the Cap is a ceiling above which your interest rate cannot go for a period of time, then a Collar is a rate of interest *below* which your interest rate cannot go for a period of time. The interest rate that you pay can fluctuate but it cannot rise above the Cap nor sink below the Collar.

Cash Back

Cash back is when the lender says, look, forget about the fixed rate and discounts and all that business, if you place your business with us we will give you 1%, 2%, 3% or (whatever the cash back deal is,) we will give you the cash back in one lump sum on the day of completion. When we talk about a mortgage 'Completing' or 'The Day of Completion', we are not talking about 25 years' time. What we are saying is that your application for the mortgage has completed, and you now have your mortgage. So your mortgage completing, is day one of your new mortgage.

Let's say you borrowed £100,000, and you are on a 5% cash back deal, then on day one of your new mortgage, on the day of completion, your lender will just send you a cheque for £5,000, or transfer it directly into your account. So that is the cash back deal.

That could be really good for a first time buyer who spends all their money raising a deposit and, now, wouldn't it be really nice if they had some money back with which to buy some furniture? Or, it could be very good for a property investor who wants to get some of the money back in order to fund the deposit or costs on their next property investment. So that is the cash back deal.

I am often asked 'What is the interest rate you pay on a cash back deal?'

Usually, if it is a full cash back deal, you go immediately onto the standard rate. In other words, whatever the incentive is, you are getting it in a lump sum, right at the beginning, instead of being spread over a period of time. There are variations and sometimes the cashback can be a small amount, perhaps sufficient to cover legal fees, etc., mixed with one of the other incentives already discussed.

Which brings me nicely onto the next point. I do not wish to give the impression that you are either offered one or the other of these incentives. These incentives can be offered as a combination, a 'mix 'n match' and, as I often say, you pay your money and you make your choice. I have seen a deal where the lender offered to fix the rate for twelve months followed by a discount for the following 2 years. They also offered a £300.00 cashback to help towards legal costs, etc. Alternatively, there have been many deals that offer 'Free Legals' as well as some of the incentives that I have already mentioned.

Early Repayment Charge (ERC)

These used to be called 'Early Redemption Penalty (ERP)' but we're not allowed to call it that anymore; now it is an 'Early Repayment Charge.
As a concept, I personally have no problems with ERC whatsoever. In effect, the lender is saying to you 'We are in business to make money. However, unless you agree to be our customer for a minimum period of time, then quite frankly it wasn't worth doing business with you in the first place. So we are prepared to give you the incentive, however, if you cease being our customer within a set period of time, then we want some or all of that incentive back.'

Now, as a concept, I think that is reasonable. Would you agree?

Where some people get very upset, is where the period of the penalty is greater than the period of the incentive. For example, if they are offering a fixed rate for two years and then state that if you get rid of your mortgage within 5 years we want some or all of the incentive back.

Some people get really annoyed with that. I have to say, anything to do with mortgages is a trade-off. The better the incentive the more severe the penalty. And other aspects within mortgages exist as a trade-off, also.

Where the period of the penalty is greater than the period of the incentive, that is referred to as 'an overhang' or as an 'extended tie-in', more usually as an 'extended tie-in'.

So, and this is important, if you were sitting down having breakfast, reading your newspaper, and flicking through the pages, you saw an advertisement from a lender, a product being promoted, and it said 'no extended tie-in', what is that telling you? It is telling you that there *is* a penalty and that the period of the penalty is the same as the deal.

You have to be careful and I want you to understand what it is you're reading. The lenders are playing games in their wording. What they want you to understand, is 'oh there's no extended tie-in, there's no penalty'. That's not what it says! If it's not extended it must be the same. No extended tie-in means there are penalties, and the penalty is the same period as the incentive.

If there were no penalties, it would say 'No penalties' as that would make for good advertising copy.
But if there were penalties it would tell you what they were, in very small print at the bottom of the advertisement.

I have to say that in the past, my clients only ever paid a penalty if they chose to. I'll repeat that. My clients only ever paid a penalty if they chose to. What do I mean by that? Well, imagine I phoned you up one day, and said:

"A new product has just come out on the market and I've been looking at your records, and I realise that if you change your mortgage to this product, you are going to be £5000 better off over the next two years. I also note that you have a £1000 Early Redemption Charge on your current mortgage. So, the reality is you are going to be £4000 better off." Given that you don't have to find the £1000 yourself (that can be financed by the new lender) and you were going to be £4000 better off – would you do it?

Of course you would. On the other hand, if I had the same conversation, that you were going to be £5000 better off, but that you had a £4,500 redemption penalty, so in reality you were only £500 better off, would you do it then? Probably not; it wouldn't be worth your time, effort or energy. And you wouldn't have thanked me for suggesting it in the first place and, so, we never would have had such a conversation.

So, if it makes sense you do it. If it doesn't make sense you don't do it. And that is why I state that my customers only paid the charge because they chose to.

But, really, what I'm getting at, in a very long-winded way, is that nobody, but nobody, is ever locked into a mortgage. The amount of times that I spoke to people, and they said, 'oh I can't do anything now I'm locked in'. It's absolute rubbish. In fact, to be locked in is illegal! One lender was sued some years ago for effectively locking someone into their mortgage by virtue of the fact that they imposed ridiculous and unfair penalties, making it unaffordable to redeem the mortgage. Consequently the courts just wiped out the penalty as it constituted an unfair contract. Nobody, but nobody, is ever locked into their mortgage. Anybody can get out of their mortgage at any time; they just might have to pay a penalty or a charge for the privilege of doing so.

Portability.

Is your mortgage portable? If your mortgage were portable, that would allow you to transfer your mortgage from one property to another, during the period of the Early Repayment Charge, without incurring that charge. But you could only do that if your mortgage was portable.

Which means the opposite is also true. If your mortgage is not portable and you wish to transfer it to another property during the Early Repayment Charge period, then the lender *will* charge you that penalty even though you are remaining with the same lender.

Let us assume that you wish to trade up and move into a bigger and better home. You can either apply for a new mortgage on the open market to fund the purchase or you might wish to retain your existing mortgage and top that up to fund the purchase of the new home. You may feel you would rather keep the mortgage you currently have as it is so much better than other mortgage products that are available to you at that time.

However, just because your mortgage is portable, there is no obligation on the part of the lender to agree to the requested increased amount; they may or may not give you the top up - that will depend upon your personal circumstances and your ability to satisfy the lender's criteria at the time you are making your application to transfer your mortgage to a different property. And they may or may not give you the top up at the same rate that you currently enjoy on your present mortgage. They might say to you 'Yes, you can transfer your existing mortgage to fund the new purchase and yes, we will agree to the top-up but the top up will be at our higher Standard Variable Rate. Or they could say 'Yes, you can transfer or Port Out (the technical jargon for transferring) your existing mortgage. Yes you can have the same rate you are currently enjoying, and yes your top up can be at the same rate, also.' And I repeat, they could say 'No' to the top up.

In fact, they are not even obliged to agree to you porting out your mortgage in the first place. They will probably require you to satisfy the criteria that is current at the time you are applying to transfer your mortgage and they could refuse the entire application.

So, all I am saying is that if your mortgage is portable and you wish to transfer it to another property during the period of the Early Repayment Charge and your lender agrees to this transfer, you will not suffer the stated Early Repayment Charge.

Therefore, if you were in that position and you are considering moving home, what my clients used to do, was phone me and say, this is what I want to do, what should I do? My answer was always the same. Phone up your current lender, tell them what it is you want to do and ask them what they are prepared to offer. Then I would look on the open market and see what I could get. If what I could get was better than what the existing lender was offering (even taking into account Early Repayment Charges and other various fees,) if it still worked out cheaper, then obviously you would go for that. If it didn't work out cheaper, then you would stick with your existing lender/product, safe in the knowledge that that was the best available to you at that time. So that's Portability and it is also another example of how you would choose to pay or not pay an Early Repayment Charge.

I do repeat, because it is important to understand, firstly, just because your mortgage is portable, does not oblige the lender to agree to the porting out of your mortgage nor to agree to topping-up or increasing your mortgage and, secondly, if your product is not portable but you still wish to use it to fund the purchase of your new property, then you are technically redeeming your mortgage and therefore, you will be required to pay the penalty. If this is the case, you might just as well be looking at the open market, including your existing lender to decide what is best for you.

Higher Lending Charge (HLC), Mortgage Insurance Premium (MIP), Mortgage Indemnity Guarantee (MIG)

So, we've had Early Repayment Charge, Early Redemption Penalties and we've discussed portability, now we come to the dreaded Higher Lending Charge, formerly called a Mortgage Insurance Premium (MIP) or Mortgage Indemnity Guarantee (MIG).

Put your hands up if you don't know what a MIP or a MIG is.
You are going to love this. It is a wonderful, wonderful concept and I'll start off by asking that you do not shoot the messenger, please.

This type of insurance policy has become so dreaded over the years that some lenders have decided to call it by a different name, to make it sound almost attractive, even desirable and have come up with such names as 'A Higher Percentage Lending Fee' and other such goodies. What I'll do is provide you with a dictionary definition of a MIP, and then I'll explain it. So, a MIP is a single premium insurance policy, which *you* pay, for the benefit of the lender and of *no* benefit to *you* whatsoever.

I'll repeat that, A MIP is a single premium insurance policy (in other words a one-off payment), which *you* pay, for the benefit of the lender, and of *no* benefit to *you* whatsoever.

Now I'll explain. Imagine there are two properties on the market each for £150,000. The person buying one of these properties wants to put down a £40,000 deposit and borrow £110,000, and the person buying the other property wants to put down a £15,000 deposit and borrow £135,000.

Would you agree that the lender lending £135,000 on a £150,000 property is taking a bigger risk than the lender who is lending £110,000 on a £150,000? Would you agree with that? Well, the MIP is merely reflecting that risk.

There is a point at which some lenders might feel uncomfortable with the level of risk you are asking them to take and feel that if you want to borrow that close to the value of the property, then they require you to take out a Mortgage Insurance Premium policy to protect them against that perceived risk.

So, let's assume now, that the person who has purchased this property, borrows his £135,000 and, as time goes on, unfortunately, things go wrong for him and, whatever the reason, he ends up having his home repossessed. Let us assume that he owed £135,000. The house eventually goes on the market, and the most that the lender is able to get is £110,000.

So, having done that, the lender has now lost £25,000. The lender will then contact the insurance company with whom the MIP was taken out at the time the mortgage completed, they will explain that they had to repossess the house, they've lost £25,000 in the transaction and they put in a claim for £25,000. The insurance company says 'no problem at all dear chap', and gives them the money less the excess on the policy. As far as the lender is concerned, they've been paid and they are then out of the picture.

The next thing that happens is a person from the insurance company knocks on your door and says 'Hi. You don't know me, but we've just laid out £25,000 on your behalf, and we would like it back please.' You're going to say, 'Oh, don't worry, because when I took out the mortgage, I also took out a MIP, so everything's okay.' And then the insurance company say, 'Ah, no, it's not okay. When you took out that policy, that was protecting the lender, it did not protect you. That policy was a single premium insurance policy, which *you* pay, for the benefit of the lender, and of *no* benefit to *you* whatsoever. You now owe us £25,000. So, cough up!'

Now, you might say that that's stupid. I've just had my house repossessed and you are asking me for £25,000! Obviously, if I had that sort of money I wouldn't be in this position in the first place, so why ask? And you would be right. So, they don't ask. Not immediately anyway. They have up to twelve years before they need to ask (not six years, as many people believe – it's different for land and property) and, provided they ask for it within twelve years, they have an indefinite period in which to pursue you.

You struggle to get your life back in order. Hopefully you can get back on track. Everything's now sweet, going nicely, and just when you think everything's okay, the insurance company knocks on your door and asks for their £25,000. So that is the wonder of the MIP. A single premium insurance policy you pay, for the protection of the lender, and of no benefit to you whatsoever.

I was often asked if the MIP was transferable and the answer is 'no'.

Can you take out a MIP for yourself? No you can't. Because no insurance company is going to give you a policy that will encourage you not to resolve your own problems. Oh, I can't afford my mortgage. I'll give the keys back; the insurance company will clear my mortgage.

However, you can take out a policy to protect your mortgage payments in the event of accident, sickness and unemployment. So if anything happens to you, your mortgage payments are paid for you, for a pre-determined period of time. You can take out a term life policy that would be set up to clear your mortgage debt in the unfortunate situation of your premature death. You can also take out permanent health insurance policy, which is not medical cover (PHI not to be confused with PMI. PMI - Private Medical Insurance is medical cover such as BUPA or AXA PPP, etc.). PHI is a policy, which will replace your income if you lose it due to accident or sickness. So you can protect your income and you can ensure your mortgage is being paid, so, in theory, there is no reason why you should ever get into arrears in the first place but you cannot take out a Mortgage Insurance Premium policy for yourself.

The irony of the MIP, is that in most cases (not all), given the reason why you are being charged the MIP in the first place, i.e. you're asking to borrow too much money, how do you fund the MIP? You borrow even more, because the lender will often just add the single payment to the new mortgage.

The rate at which the MIP cuts in varies from lender to lender. Some lenders will lend up to 100% of the purchase price without charging for a MIP. If a MIP is to be applied, it will normally cut in if you wish to borrow more than 85% of the purchase price. But there are many products over 85% where they are MIP free. But what does MIP free mean? Does it mean that a MIP is not required and, therefore it is free of MIP or does it mean there is a MIP being applied but it is free as you are not being asked to pay for it? Your mortgage adviser will tell you but in practice, it actually makes little difference to you. If there were such a policy in place, and the insurance company paid out on a claim, you would be chased by the insurance company. If there were no such policy and there was a shortfall from the forced sale, you would be chased by your lender. Either way, you would be chased.

4 Flexible Mortgage

I love Flexible Mortgages.

Actually, I use to specialise in them before they even existed; that's what got me into the world of finance in the first place, as described in my introduction.

In those days they were not called Flexible Mortgages but Aussie Mortgages, as the majority of mortgages in Australia were flexible. Mind you the majority of mortgages in South Africa are flexible; you never heard them being referred to as South African mortgages. In point of fact, I understand that the original concept was thought of by a Canadian professor of mathematics and you never heard them being called Canadian Mortgages either. As they say in Canada: 'Go figure'.

So, what makes a mortgage flexible? Is it one that does the splits?
A Flexible Mortgage is one where the lender allows you to overpay, underpay, take payment holidays and have a drawdown facility or the ability to take back out the overpayments you previously made, without the need to apply for it. Although, be careful, as each lender has its own style and definition of what constitutes a Flexible

Mortgage and you need to satisfy yourself that the features and benefits of any individual Flexible Mortgage product matches your specific needs and requirements. I have heard quite a few horror stories over the years, where the client did not realise, until it was too late, that the product did not offer the features they thought they were getting. I'll tell you one particular client's story later as this error cost her many thousands of pounds.

Very often, when I asked at my seminars, who could tell me what a Flexible Mortgage was, the first thing someone would shout out was that you can underpay it. Understand, you can only underpay your mortgage if at first you've overpaid. If you start underpaying, having never overpaid, all you have succeeded in doing is to put yourself in arrears – and that's bad news.

But a Flexible Mortgage often reflects the modern day lifestyles of many mortgage payers.
The thing that many people can't get their heads around is that it's bad enough you have to pay a mortgage, why on earth would you want to overpay it? Well, it massively reduces the overall cost of your mortgage. Also, you might have a good month or you might have a bad month. So, when you have months that are good, you can pay more into your mortgage and when the

months are bad, you can pay less. That's what I meant when I stated that it might reflect modern day lifestyles. But remember, you can only underpay if you have first overpaid.

You might think:

'Christmas is coming up. If I didn't have to pay as much on my mortgage this month, I could afford to buy an even better present for my mortgage broker (or even my family)'.

Or you might not have had so much foresight. Come January, you get your credit card statement. You read your statement and you think 'Oh my God! Did I really spend that much on my mortgage broker's Christmas present? Wouldn't it be nice, if I didn't have to pay my mortgage this month, I could clear my credit card statement instead?
So that is why you might want to overpay and underpay. You can also save money. Reduce the overall cost of purchasing your property. But there is much more to it than that.

In my seminars I used to ask a personal question of somebody. I would ask someone to volunteer and tell me what their mortgage was? I deliberately asked the question in a clumsy way. In other words how much had they mortgaged themselves for?

I remember Chris, one of the delegates and I was grateful he really entered into the spirit of things. He put his hand up and declared that he had an £84,000 mortgage.

"Chris" I said "You seem like a nice guy, and we are sitting here on a nice Sunday morning talking about mortgages, as you do. And I asked you a nice, simple question, and you lied to me. And I don't understand why you would lie to me." You should have seen his face. I continued:

"Because, in actual fact, your mortgage is not £84,000. What you have mortgaged yourself for is around about £250,000!" "Why did you lie?" I then thanked him for allowing me to have a bit of fun at his expense.

The point I was really getting at was he had done what all of us have done, myself included, fall into the trap set by the lenders, where they only want us to think and concentrate on what we've borrowed, rather than what it costs, the total amount we are destined to pay. Typically, what you are destined to pay is roughly three times the amount you borrowed. However, the lenders don't want you to think about that!

I've made your day now, haven't I?

So, the point I'm really getting to is that, if you borrowed £84,000, there is absolutely nothing I can do about that. If you borrow £84,000, you have to pay £84,000 back. But I certainly can do something about the interest you are destined to pay and that's what we're going to look at now.

As I stated, a flexible mortgage is one in which we can overpay, underpay and take payment holidays (all subject to the particular terms of your Offer of Mortgage, so you need to check it out). Interest can be calculated daily, monthly or yearly, at the discretion of the bank and they will tell you how and when they calculate the interest.

So, if you have been overpaying your mortgage, how does that benefit you? If you were overpaying an Interest Only mortgage, then the effect of the overpayment is that your outstanding balance goes down. You will remember, ordinarily, with an Interest

Only mortgage, you would expect your outstanding balance to be constant, it never goes down, but because you have been overpaying, the balance does go down. In other words, it is behaving as if it were a Repayment Mortgage.

If you overpay a Repayment Mortgage, then the outstanding balance goes down at a faster rate than originally expected and you will clear your mortgage quicker than you were originally destined to do.

So, overpayment of an Interest Only mortgage reduces the balance, on a Repayment mortgage it reduces the time.

So, let's have look at the effect of overpayment. Let's assume that this is a buy-to-let property. You can get Buy-to-Let Flexible Mortgages just as you can residential ones. Let's assume an interest only mortgage of £100,000 at a rate of interest of 6.5%. Over 20 years the monthly payment would be £541.66.

By the way, here's a question for you. If you borrow £100,000 on an Interest Only basis at 6.5% over 20 years and the monthly payment is £541.66, what would the monthly payment be if the mortgage was over 25 years?

I already covered this earlier. It would be exactly the same. What if the mortgage was over 1 year? The monthly payment would be exactly the same. In other words the monthly repayment on an interest only mortgage is exactly the same irrespective of time or the term of the mortgage. That is not true if it is a repayment mortgage. The longer the term the lower the monthly payment, and the more you will end up paying.

So, bearing in mind I have chosen a Buy-to-Let Flexible Mortgage as my example, if, over 20 years the monthly payment is £541.66 (Buy-to-Let mortgages are usually set up on an Interest Only basis), using the 130% rule (which I'll explain later), if the monthly payment is £541.66, it is reasonable to assume that the rental income is £704.16. Therefore you have a monthly profit of £162.50. Now, I know I am not taking into consideration maintenance costs, general overheads and tax liabilities, etc., and nor am I going to, as I just want to get the concept across rather than produce a business plan.

So, the monthly profit is £162.50. A flexible mortgage allows you to pay the full rental income or more if you wish or less if you wish, as a voluntary overpayment.

In actual fact, this example goes some way to underlining my own philosophy. I take the view that most of us have our particular jobs as our source of income. My philosophy is that your job provides your income and your investments provide your wealth. The two should be separated out. I know many highly paid individuals who do not have the proverbial two ha'pennies to rub together. I have also helped many people on low incomes to create incredible wealth. Your job provides your income and your investments provide your wealth.

Therefore, since you are not relying on the rent for income, what would be the effect if you just put the whole lot back into your mortgage? Bear in mind this is only a £100,000 mortgage, the effect of overpayment, which is dependent on the date of the month the rent was paid in, in relation to the date of the month the mortgage payment was paid out, over twenty years, you would save a massive £40,196.90. I'll repeat that.

You would save a massive £40,196.90.

You're supposed to go **WOW!**

That is an incredible amount considering it was only £100,000 mortgage!

Let me try to explain how so much money is saved by paying seemingly small amounts as an overpayment - not an easy task as I used to provide a full day's training to professional brokers on this very subject.

We shall stick with an Interest Only mortgage. As I have already stated, when you make your monthly payment, the outstanding balance of the mortgage remains constant; it never goes down.

For the sake of simplicity, I shall assume a £100,000 mortgage and that you decide to overpay it by £100 per month.

At the end of the first month (you haven't yet paid your first overpayment) your outstanding balance remains at £100,000. At the end of the second month, your outstanding balance is now £99,900 and so interest is calculated on this lesser amount. So you are now paying less interest. At the end of the third month the outstanding balance has been reduced to £99,800 and so you are paying even less interest than the previous month. And every month you do this, you pay less and less interest.

But, hang on a minute. If every month your balance goes down, then every month the mortgage payment should be re-calculated and your contractual monthly payment should be reducing also. And that is exactly right. But the reality is that we do not re-calculate the monthly contractual payment; we keep it as it is. So every month that you pay the original contractual amount plus an overpayment of £100, the real overpayment is more than £100. The amount by which you overpay increases every month even though you decided not to pay more than the original contracted amount plus £100 in actual payment. So, you can see, the effect of overpayment is not only exponential but it is a dual effect. The balance is reducing and you are saving substantial amounts in interest.

Now imagine you were the bank, and you are going to offer a mortgage product that's going to put into my pocket £40,000 that was originally destined for your coffers, do you think you would go out of your way to explain to me how I could best use the mortgage to ensure that I made that saving? No? And do you think you might be tempted to put some stumbling blocks in the way, in order to make sure that I don't make those savings? See, you are as cynical as I am.

That's why it is wise to seek the help of a broker who is not tied to any bank, to make sure that you get the right type of flexible mortgage to best suit your needs and also to explain how best to use it to maximise your savings.

(I was once asked if I was a tied broker. I said 'No, I had a good night's sleep, thankyou.)

For example, some lenders stipulate you can overpay by only 10% per annum during the Fixed Term Period. Now, this might be acceptable to someone who wishes to pay a little extra per month to reduce the overall cost of their mortgage. It might be unacceptable to someone who is unable to increase the monthly payments but does receive two bonuses a year and would like to use those bonuses as an overpayment and they are expected to be worth more than 10% of the annual payment. So, you see it is important to have a flexible product that allows to do what you wish to do.

I have mentioned the stumbling blocks and I also said I would tell you the unfortunate story of one of my seminar delegates. This will also be a neat introduction to Offset and Cash Account mortgages.

I seem to remember there were about two hundred and sixty delegates at this particular seminar at a hotel in Heathrow and I had just defined Flexible Mortgages, when this person put her hand up and exclaimed that she had one of these Flexible Mortgages and they're brilliant. I asked the name of her lender which then prompted me to ask whether she took advice from an independent broker or whether she discussed her needs at her local high-street branch. It was the latter. Knowing this particular lender (this was a well-known lender and as good or as bad as all the others) and having intimate knowledge of their products, I then asked if, whilst setting up this mortgage, she was also offered a non interest-earning savings account. She said she wasn't and questioned why on earth she would want a savings account that would not earn her any interest, a reasonable question.

I explained that this particular lender essentially offered a choice of two options. They offered a fully flexible mortgage where you can overpay, underpay and take a payment break and you would enjoy all of the benefits I had already explained, bar one. What she could not do was to drawdown or take back out the overpayments she previously made.

The alternative option was to have a non-interest earning savings account. They would calculate the interest owed on the mortgage by deducting the balance of the savings account from the outstanding balance of the mortgage and calculate the interest on the difference. In other words they would offset the balance of the savings account from the outstanding balance of the mortgage and calculate the interest on the difference.

As it was a savings account, of course, you could pay money in and you could take money out. However, as this money was not held in the mortgage account, it did not reduce the outstanding balance of the mortgage. So, either she could overpay, reduce the balance of the mortgage and pay considerably less interest over the term of the mortgage but cannot take back out the overpayment as a Drawdown facility or she could have the equivalent of the Drawdown facility but she wasn't reducing the balance of her mortgage debt.

Since they never even mentioned the savings account and she already knew she wanted a Flexible Mortgage, she automatically agreed to that mortgage, that is, no Drawdown.

The thing is, these products were good products and I had recommended them to many of my clients. But it was the wrong product for her and, therefore, the wrong lender for this particular individual. Her plan was to robustly save as much as she could and maximise her savings. When she was ready, she could then draw down the overpayments she made to fund the deposits on future property investments. Imagine her horror when I told her she could not automatically take out that money. It was going to cost her thousands in missed property investment opportunities. She said she would be at her branch first thing Monday morning and I wish I could have been a fly on that wall!

Offset Mortgages.

The story above already explained an Offset mortgage, as one where the savings in one account are offset against the outstanding balance of the mortgage and the interest is calculated on the difference.

There are other types of Offset accounts where all the offsetting takes place within the mortgage.

Some lenders provide a facility allowing you to create different pots, for want of a better word, and you can give each of these pots a name. My savings for a rainy day pot. My baby daughter's wedding pot. My child's university pot. And you can allocate funds into the different pots. Each month, the lender will then offset the total of all the amounts placed into the savings pots against the outstanding balance of the mortgage and then calculate the interest on the difference. This is known as 'Offsetting'.

So, just to be clear, the savings do not earn any interest but the amount of interest being paid on the mortgage account is reduced as the interest is calculated after the amount saved is deducted from the outstanding balance of the mortgage.

Cash Account Mortgages

A Cash Account Mortgage is a sophisticated version of an Offset Mortgage.

I'll start by asking you a question. If you wanted to borrow money, and you were to go to your bank for a regular bank loan, what sort of rate of interest would you expect to pay? 8%? Something around that region? If you were to make your purchase on a regular credit card, what sort of interest rate would you expect to pay then? About 14-19%? If you purchase with a store card? Too much is the answer.

What you are telling me, is that if you want to borrow money, then you would expect to pay somewhere between 7% and 30%. Is that true?

What about saving money. If you wanted to save money, what sort of interest would you expect your savings to attract? Let's start with 0%, because I've got accounts that earn nothing (or 0.1%). What's the most you're likely to get? Let's be optimistic and say 5%. So if we

were to say you could earn interest between 0 and 5% that would be reasonably accurate, yes?
And what happens to the interest that you earn? You have to pay tax on it. How do you like this as an idea? How would you like to borrow money and save money all at the same rate of interest, typically about 5.7%? Would that be attractive to you? And if I were to tell you that not only can you borrow and save at the same rate, but the interest earned on your savings are tax free, how does that appeal to you? Because that's what a cash account, bolt-on facility is. It is a Cash Account Mortgage often referred to as a CAM.

Imagine, instead of having a mortgage, you opened up a new bank account and that this was like any other account; it had a cheque book, a paying in book, credit cards, debit cards, bank statements, direct debit facilities, standing orders and everything else that you would expect from a bank account. And instead of having a mortgage, you have an overdraft. So, let's assume you wanted a £100,000 mortgage. Now instead of that, you have this new bank account with a £100,000 overdraft facility which you use to purchase your home (or clear your existing mortgage if this is your remortgage choice). Then you receive your income, and instead of going into your regular bank account it goes into this CAM account. So, once you receive your income, it immediately goes into your mortgage account, which immediately reduces the outstanding balance of your overdraft (your mortgage). As interest is usually charged daily on these accounts, whilst your income is in the account, your overdraft has been reduced which will in turn reduce the amount of interest that is going to be levied.

Now obviously, during the course of the month you will need to live and you start spending the money. As you spend it, so your overdraft increases. Nevertheless, for every day that your account is in credit or, at least, the overdraft is reduced, you are saving money on your mortgage. Therefore, it would make sense to set it up so that if you received your income on the 28th of this month, you arrange for direct debits and standing orders etc. to go out on the 27th of the following month. In other words, the longer the money stays in the account, the longer the mortgage balance is reduced, the greater will be the savings you make. And I mean substantial savings!

If you are in the habit, let's say, of putting a £100 a month away as savings for a rainy day, rather than put the £100 into a savings account, keep the £100 in your mortgage account. That way, your overdraft has been reduced by £100, and if you are on the standard variable rate of about 5.7%, there's a £100 on which you are not being charged 5.7%. Therefore, that £100 is worth 5.7% interest to you. And guess what? It's tax free. Why? Because you can't be taxed on a debt.

And if you happen to be a higher rate tax-payer, that is worth a fortune to you.

And if you happen to be self-employed, and you are in the habit of putting the money aside for tax or vat, instead of just leaving it wherever, put it into your mortgage account. I can't tell you how tasty it feels to make money out of the Inland Revenue. And it's all legal as well. And then, when you get your bill, you just write out your cheque in the normal way and pay your bill.

If there are things for which you are in the habit of paying cash - weekly shopping, petrol, etc. - instead of paying cash for those things, leave the cash in your mortgage account. That will reduce your overdraft for as long as possible and save you a fortune. Instead, purchase those items with your credit card and, when you eventually get your credit card bill, write out a cheque and pay it off in full. The last thing you want to do is to pay the interest on your credit card.

So, for me, the ideal flexible mortgage would be a CAM with the facility to create savings pots so I can see clearly between what are savings and what is mortgage debt.

So there you have it. The power of the flexible mortgage.

Warning: I believe these types of mortgages, especially the CAM, are brilliant but they do require discipline. It is too easy to create a huge saving and a drawdown facility and then spend it because you fancy a good holiday, that new car or that new kitchen you've been promising yourself. If you feel you may lack the discipline to fully exploit the benefits that these products offer, you are probably better off opting for a good quality, regular mortgage.

I thought it might be helpful if I list some questions that I was often asked at the seminars, together with the responses.

Question: Relating to Drawdown facilities, if you overpay your mortgage and later on you need some of the overpayment back, can you draw it out?

Answer: Subject to the Terms and Conditions stipulated in your original Offer of Mortgage the answer should be yes. You should be able to draw back out the overpayment and, of course, returning to my earlier cynicism, it makes perfect sense; it is good for the lender to provide this facility and allow you to borrow back that money as they do not lose as much when you do that. However, you do need to satisfy yourself at the time you receive your offer of mortgage and before you commit to that particular mortgage product, that it offers the features you require, including the ability to take back out the overpayments that you previously made, if that is what you want.

Question: Are there any other ways to maximise the benefits of these mortgages, you know, the tricks of the trade?

Answer: If you qualify for a larger mortgage than you actually need, borrow the most amount available to you. Whatever is surplus to your immediate needs, pay that back as a lump sum overpayment into your mortgage. You can either choose to pay the monthly contractual amount for this enlarged mortgage, with all the associated benefits (of overpayment) we have already discussed or you can ask the lender to re-calculate the monthly payment to reflect the reduced outstanding balance. What this means is you now have an emergency fund available to you within a matter of days of you requesting it. It is usually just a matter of a phone call.

Also, if you wish to make a major purchase you can decide whether to pay cash by making use of the drawdown facility or borrow the money by way of personal loan or credit card. For example, if you have a zero rate credit card, it would make more sense making your purchase with that card and leave the balance of your mortgage reduced, saving you 5.7% (if that happens to be the current rate of your mortgage interest). If your credit card is charging, say 19% interest, you would be better off still making the purchase with the card, so that you enjoy the extra protection provided by the Consumer Credit Act for purchases over £100 and then drawdown the money to clear the card before the end of the month, to avoid paying their rate of interest. If you have taken out the maximum available to you, such that you have no further drawdown facility available, but you have a zero balance on your cards, then you have the satisfaction of knowing that the credit facility on the cards is still available to you as an emergency fund, should you need it.

I had some clients that were able to create such a substantial drawdown facility that they were able to use this to purchase more properties. Knowing they had this drawdown facility, they turned themselves into cash buyers which meant they could negotiate really good prices. Once they purchased the property, they could arrange a mortgage on that property and then pay that amount back into their CAM mortgage, ready to do the same thing all over again. Think about it. They could possibly negotiate purchasing a property at 30% below market value, because they are cash buyers and can move quickly, and then arrange a mortgage of 75% LTV (hopefully, you're understanding the jargon, now). That means not only did they purchase a property for nothing but they probably had enough left over to treat themselves to a nice little holiday for doing such a great deal. Not bad, eh?

There is something else worthy of consideration. If you are in the position to clear your mortgage debt completely, you may wish to leave a balance of £1.00. That way, you effectively have a £1.00 mortgage and a lender who is looking after your Property Deeds at no charge to you other than the interest on £1.00. If a mortgage of £1.00 is impractical, make it £10.00, instead.

Question: Is that the only way to obtain a Drawdown facility?

Answer: Some lenders allow you to set up a Drawdown facility at the time of applying for your mortgage even if the mortgage product itself is not flexible. You access some of it or all of it as and when you need it. Some lenders put a time limit as to how long the facility remains available to you. Some lenders take the view that as they have to set aside funds to be available for you to draw down, they will charge you a nominal fee for the facility and other lenders make no such charge.

So, that is flexible mortgages in all its different forms. They are a very, very powerful product. The amount of money you can save can be absolutely phenomenal.

Important. There are many considerations and variations when looking at Flexible Mortgages and I would strongly urge you to seek professional advice from a Whole of Market adviser before

accepting a mortgage product. The Terms and Conditions, the features, facilities and processes are forever changing and it is essential that you satisfy yourself that the product you are considering offers you what you want and allows you to do exactly what you want it to do for you. **Not all Flexible Mortgages are the same!**

5 Off On A Slight Tangent & Amusing Anecdotes

To lighten the load for a while, I thought I would mention some true and amusing stories.

It is important to understand, that the mortgage industry is a totally upside down business. If they have any sense of logic, and I suspect they don't, but if they do, it is totally different to your understanding and my understanding of logic. In fact, it was quite often the case, when talking to a complaining client that I would respond by stating the trouble with their thinking is it is logical and banks don't think that way. And believe me, I was being serious. Very often, as an intermediary, I use to think of myself as the link between our world and theirs.

I once had a phone call from my office, telling me that they had received a phone call from a lender, asking me to phone my client and ask them why they had a history of debt. I said that I was not prepared to ask my client that question and, instead, instructed the office to phone the lender back and tell them the reason that my client had a history of debt, is that he spent more money than he had. My colleague asked if I was serious. I said 'Yes, absolutely'. 'Okay' she said in that tone of voice that questioned my sanity. Ten minutes later she phoned me back, giggling and said:

"I phoned the bank and told them what you said, word for word and the voice at the other end said ah, okay, thank you and put the phone down." That mortgage went through without any problems.

Strangely enough, within a week of that, I received a letter from another bank regarding another client, asking me to explain why my client had a history of arrears. I wrote back stating my client did not have a history of arrears. However, due to the pressures of modern day living, they sometimes paid late. That application also went through without any problem at all.

So sometimes, you need somebody who has a little bit more experience and understanding about lenders, how they work and how they think, in order to actually achieve what it is you want to achieve. They are obliged to ask the question and we have to supply an answer. I suppose there's some logic there, isn't there?

Question: Was I serious about loyalty being misplaced or was I just being cynical for the sake of being cynical?

Answer: Actually, I don't really consider myself cynical. I am factual and just tell it the way it is. Let me give you an example.

Imagine you run a newsagent and you get an offer from your tobacco supplier. It reads 'Buy these cigarettes which normally sell for £9.00 for 20, you can sell them for £7.00 and still make the same profit.'

This offer is so good, that there is a quota. All that you can have is 5000 cigarettes.

So, question 1. Are you going to take your full quota? Obviously you are, because you know, at that price, you can sell them in no time at all. 5000 at a substantially reduced price, you can sell them in a day, probably in half an hour.

The question now is what are you going to do with these cigarettes? Are you going to stand them high on the counter with a sign saying cigarettes at reduced prices whilst stocks last? Or might you think to yourself, 'Hang on a moment, I've only got 5000. I know I'm going to sell these in no time at all, why should I sell these to people I'm never going to see again? Why should I sell them to all the passing trade? What I'll do is, I'll stick them under the counter and only sell them to my regular customers.' Which are you more likely to do?

Obviously you are going to stick them under the counter. You can only sell them once and you would rather it was your loyal customers that got the benefit of such a great offer. So, what you're telling me, is that you would reward loyalty. Do the banks do this? Absolutely not.

Imagine that you are having you're breakfast, and you are glancing through your newspaper, and you see a mortgage product being advertised and you think 'Ooh, that looks good. I'll have some of that'. So, off you go to your lender. 'Hi, I've been your customer for 10 years, I'm a very, very good customer and I've never missed a payment. I've paid my mortgage month in month out on time, full amount, I've never ever missed a payment. I'm a really good customer of yours. I was reading about this mortgage product, and I think it's fantastic. I want it. And the lender says, 'oh no. That's not for you, that's only for the new customers.'

The new customers are getting the best deals, and who's subsidising them? You are, the good old regular customers, those on the Standard Variable Rate. So, the question you have to ask yourself is:
Are you happy to stick with your lender out of some misguided sense of loyalty and subsidise somebody else's great deal, or would you rather find a different lender who is offering something much better than you currently have and let somebody else subsidise you?

You see, what I'm really getting at, is if you haven't changed your mortgage in the last two or three years, you should certainly be investigating it because the chances are you can save a lot of money. We all want to learn how to make money and the first rule about making money is put your own house in order first and capitalise on what you already have. Then you can move forward to other new and exciting matters.

Question: Is it true that interest rates are generally cheaper in Europe, and how do you get a Euro mortgage?

Answer: Are interest rates generally cheaper in Europe? Sometimes yes, sometimes no. Can you get a Euro mortgage? Yes. Is it advisable? Probably not. What I would say is that our mortgage market is probably the most sophisticated and regulated in the world, and my feelings are that if any country wants to change their mortgage system, it is ours they ought to adopt and not the other way round. Plus, you have complications with currency exchange rates and such like. So, as a general principle, I feel it is better to have a mortgage in the currency of the country in which the property is located.

I shall be writing another book on how to invest in property but, for the time-being I just want to make a couple of points.

130% Rule

Earlier on, I referred to the 130% rule as it applies to Buy-to-Let mortgages. As a general rule, a lender will require that the rent exceeds the monthly mortgage payment by 130% and I call this the 130% rule. If you want the jargon, it is referred to as the lender's 'Stress Rate'. I like to work within the 130% rate (even if a lender's actual stress rate is lower, as it provides a margin of safety). Imagine you are thinking of investing in a property, you have done your research and you have learnt that the achievable rent is £1300 per month. If you divide this by 130% (or 1.3), it is reasonable to assume that the monthly mortgage payment will be £1000. So, just from knowing what the achievable rent is, I know approximately what my mortgage payment is going to be even before I have approached a lender.

To take this one stage further, if you now know what your monthly mortgage payment is and if you knew what rate of interest to apply, bearing in mind that, as this relates to Buy-to-Let, it is reasonable to assume that you will have an Interest Only mortgage, you can calculate how much you borrowed. Most people say I want to borrow this much, how much is the monthly payment? I am saying, no. I know what the monthly payment is, how much did I borrow? If you want your mortgage to represent, say, 75% LTV, you can then calculate what a 100% is. And once you know what a 100% is you now know the most you are prepared to pay, irrespective of how much the vendor is asking for the property. I prefer to use an interest rate of 6% as I feel that the combination of a stress rate of 130% and a notional rate of interest of 6% provides enough of a margin of error to satisfy my risk management requirements (of course, if interest rates in general increase, then I would increase my notional rate, also).

Example:

A property is on the market for £360,000 and we'll assume that is a reasonable asking price for this type of property in this area. I do my research and establish that the achievable rental income is £1,400 per month. That is all I need to know as far as calculating the amount I am prepared to pay is concerned.

$$
\begin{aligned}
1400 / 130\% &= 1077 \\
1077 / 6\% \times 12 &= 215400 \\
215400 / 75\% &= 287200
\end{aligned}
$$

I now know that even though the property is on the market for £360,000, the most I am prepared to pay is £287200. That is the 130% rule.

Moreover, as I have used a mathematical calculation to determine the exact amount I am prepared to pay for a property, I am able to negotiate with more conviction and more robustly than would be the case if I were merely plucking a figure out of thin air and chancing my luck in the hope they would accept it.

6 Capital Raising, Releasing Equity and Debt Consolidation

I have grouped these together as they are essentially the same thing. But first a warning:

Releasing equity should not be confused with Equity Release Mortgages. I shall cover Equity Release Mortgages in the next section.

It is often the case that whilst you are applying for a new, cheaper mortgage, you may wish to avail yourself of extra cash to fund a major purchase such as a new home extension, a new kitchen or bathroom or even a good holiday. In fact, it could be, that the main motivation for changing your mortgage is to raise funds and, whilst you're at it, if you can get a better quality mortgage, so much the better.

So, Capital Raising or releasing equity is the act of borrowing more than is required to clear your existing mortgage in order to leave you with a surplus of money. If you are raising cash in order to clear debt then that is referred to as 'Debt Consolidation'. Some people refer to capital raising and debt consolidation. Essentially they are one and the same thing; it just means you are raising enough to clear your debts and an extra amount for you to use however you wish.

There is an important point to ponder if you are raising capital to consolidate unsecured debt such as credit cards, personal loans, etc. It very often makes sense to consolidate debt in this manner. It usually results in paying less interest, reducing your total monthly expenditure and, sometimes, protecting what otherwise might become, a damaged credit status. In that sense, debt consolidation is a good thing.

The downside is that if your mortgage is for twenty-five years, you are effectively converting short-term debts into long-term debts. Whilst you would have reduced your monthly expenditure, you might well have increased the overall cost of those debts. Now, debt consolidation may still be desirable and the best advice in your circumstances; I just feel that one should enter into this arrangement with one's eyes open.

The other thing to realise is that you have converted what was an unsecured debt into a secured debt. However, I think, since the Government made the putting of a charge on one's home easier, where their customers default on their account, than was previously the case (something that I think the Government got totally wrong, is unfair to borrowers and too advantageous to lenders), this fact of converting an unsecured debt to a secured debt perhaps becomes of lesser importance when considering debt consolidation but one should be aware of it nonetheless.

7 Equity Release/Lifetime Mortgages & Home Reversion

Let me say upfront that I love the concept of these mortgages and I think we shall see a lot more of them over the next few years.

However, they were not so good when they first came on to the market; in fact they were pretty disgusting. To this day, if you are considering such a mortgage and you mention it to a well-intentioned friend down at the pub, he might well tell you to steer well clear and don't touch them with the proverbial barge pole and this will be based on how they used to be and not as they are now. These mortgages used to be so bad that they became and still are the most regulated product of all mortgage products. Anybody advising on these products has to pass specific exams designed purely for them and then be supervised in the first few months before they are fully qualified to proceed. They are totally ethical products that satisfy a specific and genuine need.

Usually available to those over the age of fifty-five, Equity Release Mortgages are intended for those who are asset rich and cash poor. It is, unfortunately, often the case that a person has worked hard all his/her life to buy their home, they own something that is worth many thousands of pounds (the asset) and yet have little or no standard of living because of a lack of cash or income.

The Equity Release Mortgage is a facility for senior citizens (starting from the age of fifty-five) that allows them to draw a percentage of the value of their property as a cash fund. I never did qualify for advising on these products but, as I understand it, you can choose to take out money as a lump sum, you can take out money as a monthly income or you can take it as mixture of both.

You can choose whether to have an interest only monthly payment or you can choose to have no monthly payment whatsoever, with the interest 'Rolled Up'. In other words, you pay nothing in respect of monthly mortgage payments. Instead, you allow the interest to accumulate and when you move into a nursing home or decide to join the big landlord in the sky, your home would be sold and the debt and the interest that accrued would be cleared from the proceeds of the sale of the property. Whatever is left, would go back to your estate.

Given the nature of the product and what it does for the quality of life for the one borrowing the money (the Mortgagee), I do not feel the rate of interest on these products is exorbitant. Given that I believe the statistical rate at which the value of property doubles will be maintained (statistically, properties in the UK double every 7.2 years which equates to 10% per annum), the value of a property is likely to increase at a greater rate than the mortgage debt increases, although, of course, no guarantees can be given in this regard.

However, one of the features of these mortgage products is that if it is unavoidable that the property is sold at a time when the property is in negative equity, then the lender is obliged to wipe out the remaining debt. So there may be no inheritance but there would be no debt either.

These mortgages can be used to raise capital on unencumbered properties (i.e. the property is free of mortgage and currently owned outright), it can be used to clear an existing, traditional mortgage (possibly a solution if you have an Interest Only mortgage and no means or repayment vehicle with which to clear the mortgage debt, at the end of the term) and it can be used to purchase a property. Of course, the availability of the mortgage, like any other mortgage, is subject to satisfying the criteria of the lender but, unlike ordinary mortgages, they are not subject to status as it is supplied based on the value of your property and not on your ability to clear the debt.

8 Self-Build Mortgages

Many people like the idea of building their own home, as they end up with exactly what they want. Whether one is intending to do all the work themselves and only call in other specialist professionals if and when required or one calls in a project manager to oversee the work done by others or employs a contractor to take over the entire project, unless you have a large amount of cash sitting in your bank account, you will require a special form of financing. One requires funding in advance of the work to be done rather than after the work has been done and a Self-Build mortgage provides this specialist form of financing. You cannot use a standard mortgage to fund this type of project.

The main difference between a Self-Build mortgage and a standard residential mortgage is that the funds are released in stages rather than as a single lump sum. This reduces both the lender's risk and that of the borrower, by ensuring the money is spent as planned and one doesn't run out of money half way through the project. As a general rule, the first tranche of money is released when the land is purchased and the second when the foundations are laid. A further payment is released when the property is completed up to eaves level. The final payments will be made when the building is weatherproof and ready for decorating, with the last instalment paid on completion.

Stage payments are usually only paid out once a valuer has visited the site and confirmed satisfactory completion of that stage of the build. There are many different types of these mortgage products and I feel it is important to seek advice from a broker that is both knowledgeable and experienced in dealing with these types of products.

One of the good things about self-build is that, at the time of writing at least, you only pay Stamp Duty on the purchase of the land but not on the property and it is exempt from vat.

It is reasonable to assume that the value of the completed property is more than the cost of building it. Once the property is completed, it should then qualify for a normal residential mortgage that can be used to clear the Self Build Mortgage, as always, subject to satisfying the criteria and terms and conditions of the lender.

9 Bridging Loans

Bridging loans are a specialised form of lending designed to solve a problem. Imagine you have decided to move home, perhaps to accommodate a growing family and you intend to sell your existing home and buy your new home simultaneously.

Just as you were about to exchange contracts on both transactions and become legally bound to both selling and buying, your buyer notifies you of a problem that prevents him from exchanging contracts at that time or, worse still, he has changed his mind and does not wish to proceed with his purchase. You now have a dilemma and a problem to solve. You need the money from the sale of your property in order to be in a position to honour your agreement with your vendor, the owner of the property you are hoping to buy. Now that your purchaser has pulled out, you are concerned that if you postpone exchanging contracts on your purchase as a consequence, you may lose your purchase and end up having wasted your money on such expenses as legal fees, disbursements, lender's valuation fee and a Homebuyer's report to name but a few and then have to start the whole process from scratch.

Equally, you don't want to exchange contracts on your purchase only to find that you do not have the funds to enable you to complete on the purchase because of your inability to exchange contracts on your sale and derive the benefit of the funds you would have received from the proceeds of the sale. The last thing you want is to be in breach of your contract to purchase. You could be sued for thousands and many people have become bankrupt and lost everything as a result of this situation. Alternatively, you could take out a Bridging Loan that will enable you to purchase the property without having first sold your own property. You will clear the Bridging Loan later on from the proceeds of the sale of your property.

However, there is a danger. Firstly, Bridging Loans can be expensive. Secondly, what if it takes longer than you anticipate to find a new buyer and to complete on your sale? What if you are unable to sell the property for the same amount that the original purchaser agreed to pay? What if you just cannot sell the property at a price that you are prepared to accept?

Bridging loans definitely can be the answer to a problem but they need to be treated with caution and proper professional advice should be obtained before entering into such an arrangement.

In Conclusion

Firstly, I would like to give you my reason for being so excited by property as a vehicle for investment. I can't think of anything that provides the Power of Leverage in as powerful a way as property.

Imagine you had £100,000 to invest and you invested that in Stocks and Shares. Now imagine those stocks and shares went up in value by 10% in the first year. And, for the sake of this example, let us assume that there are no costs, no commissions, no tax to pay, only pure profit. That means you have made £10,000 in your first year. I think you will agree that that was a good investment by anybody's standards. You would be delighted with that, wouldn't you and rightly so?

Now take the same £100,000 and use that to fund deposits for the purchase of £400,000 worth of properties (75% LTV) and imagine those properties have gone up in value by 10% in the first year. Given that you are not paying for the mortgage payments, they are being funded by the rents you collect, you would have made not £10,000 but a whopping £40,000!!! Now do you see why I get so excited by property as a vehicle for investment? And if you really understand mortgages and how they work, there is so much you can do to maximise your profits still further. I shall expand on this and much more in my book about property investment.

Lastly, I would like to take the opportunity to thank you for taking the time to read this book. I am very aware that mortgages are a boring subject (even though I love them). Nobody really wants one, everybody prays for the day they can be rid of them and yet, everyone wants one for what a mortgage can do for them. I hope you agree that the knowledge and information that I have imparted has been in a light-hearted, easy-to-understand and, dare I say, even enjoyable format. Whether you are a first-time buyer, someone who has had several mortgages or someone who is entering or already part of the mortgage industry I wish you luck and success in every aspect of your life.

Please follow me, read my blogs, newsletters and information sheets. Feel free to congratulate me or berate me, as you see fit. I enjoy new relationships, maintaining existing relationships, renewing old relationships and helping out wherever I can and the best and only way to do that is through effective communication.

10 Glossary of Terms & Jargon Buster

Additional Borrowing

A term used to describe increasing the borrowing to release some or all of the available equity in a property.

Advance

The total amount the lender is lending including the amount of the mortgage and any fees, costs and charges that might be added to the mortgage amount.

Annual Percentage Rate (APR)

APR is a rate of interest that lenders are required to quote to provide a better opportunity for borrowers to compare different products from either the same lender or from other lenders, on a like-for-like basis, so they can make an informed choice as to what is the best product to suit their circumstances.

Arrangement Fee

A fee that some lenders will charge to set up the loan.
Some lenders will allow the Arrangement Fee to be added to the loan and is only chargeable provided the mortgage completes. Often, low rate deals have higher arrangement fees, sometimes making them worse than higher rate deals.

Arrears

One is said to be in arrears when one month or more of mortgage payments have been missed.

Bank of England Base Rate (BoEBR)

This is the rate which is set on a monthly basis by the Monetary Policy Committee (MPC) of the Bank of England and is the rate that it charges for its lending.

Benefit Period

The period of time from the commencement of the mortgage to the date that an incentive or special rate comes to an end.

Booking Fee

Usually a non-refundable fee charged by some lenders on some of their products to reserve a particular product. This is usually paid up-front at the time the mortgage application is submitted to the lender for their consideration. Some lenders may charge a Booking Fee in addition to an Arrangement Fee. It is unusual for a Booking Fee to be added to the mortgage advance and it is usual, especially where there is a Booking Fee, that if an Arrangement Fee is being charged, the Arrangement Fee be added to the mortgage advance. The Booking Fee is usually non-refundable.

Bridging Loan

A Bridging Loan is usually a short-term loan, lent by a bank, to cover an interval between two transactions, typically the buying of one house and the selling of another.

Building Survey

Not to be confused with a Valuation, it is wise for a purchaser to instruct an independent survey to provide a report on the state of the building and other associated issues, prior to committing oneself by exchanging contracts.

Buy-to-Let

A style of mortgage designed specifically to fund the purchase of a property with the intention of letting it out rather than living in it. The legal requirements and, therefore, the Terms & Conditions of such mortgages are different to those of standard residential mortgages.

CAM (Cash Account Mortgage)

A specialist feature of a Flexible Mortgage that provides a bank (current) account where the balance in the account is offset against the outstanding balance of a mortgage for the purpose of calculating the amount of mortgage interest to be charged.

Capital & Interest Mortgage (Repayment)

A Capital & Interest Mortgage, more commonly called a Repayment Mortgage, is a mortgage structured so that the monthly payments are designed to pay all the interest and clear the mortgage debt by the end of the term of the mortgage.

Capped

A style of incentive where the interest rate cannot rise above a pre-determined rate of interest for a fixed period of time, irrespective of how much interest rates increase on the open market during the Benefit Period.

Cash Account Mortgage (CAM)

A specialist feature of a Flexible Mortgage that provides a bank (current) account where the balance in the account is offset against the outstanding balance of a mortgage for the purpose of calculating the amount of mortgage interest to be charge.

Cashback

A style of incentive where a lender agrees to either pay a fixed sum of money or an amount of money expressed as a percentage of the amount borrowed. This money is paid on the day the mortgage completes (i.e. day one of the new mortgage).

Chargeable Rate

Also known as a Notional Rate, a Chargeable Rate, is an imaginary rate of interest, used by some lenders in conjunction with their Stress Rate, to determine the amount they are prepared lend on a Buy-to-Let property.

Chartered Surveyor

A Chartered Surveyor is a professional person, registered with the Royal Institution of Chartered Surveyors (RICS), to provide an impartial opinion on the state and condition of a property as well as a variety of diverse property related issues.

Collared

A restriction ensuring the interest rate cannot fall below a pre-determined rate of interest for a period of time, irrespective of how much interest rates decrease on the open market.

Completion

The point at which the money is released to either purchase a property or remortgage it. In Scotland this is known as Settlement.

Completion Fee

A fee to cover the cost of electronically transferring the mortgage funds to the borrower.

Conclusion of Missives

The point at which both buyer and seller are legally bound to the purchase (Scotland only). The English equivalent of Exchange of Contracts.

Conveyance

The legal document which transfers ownership of unregistered freehold land, in England and Wales.

Conveyancing

The work associated with the creating of the legal document which transfers ownership of unregistered freehold land, in England and Wales.

Deferred Interest

Allows a borrower to make payments of the interest element of a Repayment Mortgage at a later date. However, the mortgage debt will increase during the deferred period. E.g. deferred for six months means that whilst a reduced amount is being paid, the interest on the amount not being paid is being added on each month.

Deposit Amount

The difference between the purchase price and the amount being borrowed to finance the purchase.

Disbursements

Disbursements are fees a solicitor or conveyancer has to pay to others on behalf of the client e.g. Stamp Duty Land Tax, Land Registry Fees, Search Fees.

Discount

Is an incentive where the rate of interest is set at a specific percentage below the lender's Standard Variable Rate (SVR) for a pre-determined period of time e.g. if the lender has an SVR of 6% and the discount is 2.5%, you would actually pay at a rate of 3.5%.

Early Repayment Charge (ERC)

A charge levied by a lender to the customer for paying off all or some of a mortgage over and above the contractual amount, within a pre-determined period of time. Usually linked in to an incentive provided at the time the mortgage completed.

Early Repayment Penalty (ERP)

Regulations state that one can no longer refer to these as penalties but is the same definition as Early Repayment Charge (ERC).

Electronic Transfer

The method by which a mortgage advance is paid to the conveyancer.

Endowment Mortgage

An Endowment Mortgage is an Interest Only mortgage where an Endowment policy is set up as the means to pay the mortgage debt by the due date, at the end of the term of the mortgage.

Endowment Policy

Is a 'With Profits' or 'Unit Linked' policy, with a life insurance element, designed to create a fund sufficient to clear the mortgage debt at the end of the term of an Interest Only mortgage.

Equity

The positive difference between the value of a property and the amount of any outstanding mortgages and loans secured against it.

Equity Release

Borrowing money based on the positive difference between the value of a property and the amount of any outstanding loans secured against it.

Equity Release Mortgage

Is a mortgage designed for people from the age of 55 and over who find themselves asset rich and cash poor. There are various schemes and they enable senior citizens to receive a lump-sum payment or a monthly income or a mixture of both. They are available only from people specifically qualified to provide advice on this type of mortgage product.

Extended Tie-In

Also referred to as an 'Overhang', it is where the period of an Early Repayment Charge (ERC) is greater than the period of a mortgage incentive.

Fee Saver

Fee Saver is a style of incentive where a lender provides a product that does not have Arrangement Fees or Booking Fees. This may be in addition to other incentives that a lender may offer.

First Time Buyer

A First Time Buyer is a person who has not previously owned a property or has not owned a property for the previous twelve months.

Fixed Rate

A style of incentive where a lender offers an agreed rate of interest that will never increase or decrease for a pre-determined period of time, irrespective of what is happening to interest rates in general.

Flexible

A mortgage with special additional features e.g. offering the facility to overpay and underpay the monthly payments, making lump sum payments (overpayments), temporarily stopping payments (payment holiday).

Freehold

Owning land or property outright, with the responsibility for all maintenance and repairs.

Full Structural Survey

A full structural report is provided by one or more expert professionals, reporting on the state and condition of a property. Most purchasers of property tend to rely on a lesser Home Buyer's Report as this is less expensive and usually regarded as satisfactory.

Gazumping

Gazumping is an unsavoury act where a vendor has agreed a price with a purchaser and then sells the property to a third party for a higher price unless the original purchaser agrees to match or better that price.

Gazundering

Gazundering is an unsavoury act where a purchaser has agreed a price with a vendor and then offers a reduced price just before the exchange of contracts or threatens not to exchange.

Guarantor

A third party entering into a legally binding contract to pay a mortgage if the main applicant fails to do so (often a parent for a first time buyer will act as a guarantor), providing the lender with extra security.

Higher Lending Charge

Also known as a Mortgage Indemnity Guarantee or a Mortgage Insurance Premium, it is an insurance policy required by some lenders on some products, where the lender is being asked to lend an amount close to the value of the property. This exposes the lender to greater risk and they require an insurance policy to protect them from this enhanced level of risk.

Home Buyer's Report

A Home Buyer's Report is a lesser form of a full, structural survey. It is usually provided by a Chartered Surveyor and reports on every aspect of a building that is visible for inspection and does not require the removal or exposing of anything in order to make the inspection possible.

Home Reversion Mortgage

Is a style of an Equity Release Mortgage where the owner sells a percentage of the property but retains the right to live there.

Homebuy

A government sponsored scheme that assists existing tenants, keyworkers and those in need, to get on the property ladder.

House in Multiple Occupation (HMO's)

A property is a House in Multiple Occupation (HMO) if both of the following apply:
- At least three tenants live there, forming more than one household.
- A toilet, bathroom or kitchen facilities are shared with other tenants.

A property is a large HMO if all of the following apply:
- It is at least three storeys high.

- It has at least five tenants living there, forming more than one household.
- A toilet, bathroom or kitchen facilities are shared with other tenants.

Interest Only Mortgage

An Interest Only mortgage is one where the monthly payment only covers the cost of the interest and does not reduce the amount of the original mortgage debt.

ISA Mortgage

Is a government backed savings policy set up to create a fund sufficient to clear the mortgage debt at the end of the term of an Interest Only mortgage.

Islamic Mortgage

A style of mortgage conforming to the requirements of the law of the Quran where the charging of interest is forbidden. The two most common are **Ijara** under which the bank buys the property for the client and the client then leases it back from the bank, making monthly payments and **Murabaha,** where the bank buys the property and the client then buys it back immediately for a higher price, paying off the debt over a specified term e.g. 15 years.

Joint Tenancy

A style of ownership where the owners (two or more) are said to each own a 100% of the property. Conveyancers more often register a property at Land Registry on this basis as upon the death of either party, ownership passes entirely and automatically to the survivor, without the need for a will. There are advantages and disadvantages to holding a property as Joint Tenancy and professional advice should be sought.

Key Facts Illustration (KFI)

A document that must be provided to the applicant for a mortgage and provides all the key information needed when choosing a mortgage. It facilitates making comparisons between different mortgage products with different lenders.

Key Features

A document that must be provided by a mortgage broker and provides details of charges made by the broker, rates and fees, as well as other information.

Lease

A document which grants possession of a property for a fixed period of time and sets out the obligations of both parties, landlord and tenant, such as payment of rent, repairs and insurance.

Leasehold

Leasehold is a way of owning land or property for a set period of time after which possession reverts to the Freeholder. The Freeholder has the responsibility for all maintenance and repairs.

Let to Buy

More commonly referred to as shared ownership, it allows for the buying of only a part of a property and paying rent on the remainder. For some people this is the only way to get a foot on the property ladder and is the first step to whole property ownership.

Let to Buy Mortgage

Remortgaging and capital raising with a Buy to Let mortgage on a residential property with the intention of renting out the residential home and regarding that as an investment property. The capital raised is used to fund or
part-fund the deposit required for a new residential property.

LIBOR

London Inter-Bank Offered Rate. The wholesale rate of interest that the banks charge each other for loans.

Lifetime Mortgages

An alternative name for Equity Release mortgages and Home Reversion mortgages.

Limits of Exposure

The limits to which a lender is prepared to expose itself to risk such as:

- The maximum number of mortgages it will provide to a single customer.
- The maximum a lender is prepared to lend to a customer based either on total borrowing or total value of properties.
- The maximum number of properties a lender is prepared to lend on, in a given estate or area.

Loan

Sometimes referred to as the advance, this is the actual amount of money that has been provided as a loan.

Loan To Value (LTV)

LTV is the mortgage amount expressed as a percentage of the value of a property.

Missives

Scotland only. The formal written offer to purchase and the acceptance.

Mortgage

A mortgage is where a charge is placed upon land or other property as security for the lender. In the event of default, a lender has the security knowing it can sell the land or property in question to recover its money. Hence, the legal requirement for lenders and those associated with offering mortgages and mortgage advice to state:

YOUR HOME MAY BE REPOSSESSED IF YOU DO NOT KEEP UP REPAYMENTS ON YOUR MORTGAGE.

Mortgage Deed

The contract between the lender and the borrower. It sets down the legal obligations of the borrower and the rights of the lender.

Mortgage Indemnity Guarantee (MIG)

Also known as a Mortgage Insurance Premium or a Higher Lending Charge, it is an insurance policy required by some lenders on some products, where the lender is being asked to lend an amount close to the value of the property. This exposes the lender to greater risk and they require an insurance policy to protect them from this enhanced level of risk.

Mortgage Insurance Premium

Also known as a Mortgage Indemnity Guarantee or a Higher Lending Charge, it is an insurance policy required by some lenders on some products, where the lender is being asked to lend an amount close to the value of the property. This exposes the lender to greater risk and they require an insurance policy to protect them from this enhanced level of risk.

Mortgagee

The lender or the mortgage provider

Mortgagor

The borrower. The person taking out the mortgage

Negative Equity

The difference between the value of a property and the amount of any outstanding mortgages and loans secured against it, where the total outstanding balance or balances of such loans is greater than the value of the property.

Non-conforming

Also known as sub-prime and non-status, non-conforming is a mortgage made available to those with a poor credit history, perhaps with, but not necessarily, County Court Judgements (CCJs) or for those who have been bankrupt or in arrears. Rates are likely to be higher than those available in the market as a whole and/or the Loan to Value may be restricted.

Non-status

Also known as sub-prime and non-conforming, non-status is a mortgage made available to those with a poor credit history, perhaps with, but not necessarily, County Court Judgements (CCJs) or for those who have been bankrupt or in arrears. Rates are likely to be higher than those available in the market as a whole and/or the Loan to Value may be restricted.

Notional Rate (Chargeable Rate)

Also known as a Chargeable Rate, a Notional Rate is an imaginary rate of interest, used by some lenders in conjunction with their Stress Rate, to determine the amount they are prepared to lend on a Buy-to-Let property.

Offset Mortgage

An Offset Mortgage is either a savings facility built into a mortgage or a separate savings account, where the balance of the savings is deducted from the mortgage debt. The interest charged on the mortgage is calculated on the difference. This is instead of calculating earned interest on savings.

Outstanding Balance

A statement of how much is left owing on a debt, including a mortgage, at any given time. When in the context of a mortgage, the outstanding balance should not be taken as the amount necessary to clear the mortgage debt as there may be additional costs and charges associated with fully redeeming a mortgage.

Overhang

Also referred to as an 'Extended Tie-In', it is where the period of an Early Repayment Charge (ERC) is greater than the period of a mortgage incentive.

Payment Shock

The feeling you might have when you come to the end of a deal and this month's mortgage payment is much higher than last month's. This is referred to as Payment Shock

Pension Scheme Mortgage

A Pension Scheme Mortgage is an Interest Only mortgage where a pension policy is set up as the means to pay the mortgage debt by the due date, at the end of the term of the mortgage.

Pied-à-Terre

Directly translated from the French, this means "foot on the ground". In property jargon, it refers to a property kept for temporary, secondary or occasional occupation.

Portable

A feature of a mortgage product that allows the transferring of an existing mortgage product to a new or different property during the period of an Early Repayment Charge, without suffering that charge.

Porting

The process or act of transferring an existing mortgage product to a new property. All of the terms and conditions of the existing mortgage remain the same but the mortgage is moved onto the new property being purchased.

Public Liability Insurance

In relation to a property, this is an insurance policy that is usually a feature within a Buildings policy that covers the property owner in case of an accident incurred whilst on the protected property e.g. a roof tile slips off the roof and hits the postman as he is delivering the post.

Redemption Administration Fee

A fee charged by the lender for releasing the legal charge over a property following full repayment of a mortgage.

Redemption Statement

Issued by an existing lender, it shows exactly the amount necessary to pay, including all fees, charges, costs and interest owing, to pay off the mortgage debt, completely.

Remortgage

The process of applying for or taking out a new mortgage product, either with the same lender or a new lender, to replace your existing mortgage product, without moving home.

Repayment Mortgage

More correctly called a Capital & Interest mortgage, a Repayment Mortgage is one where the monthly payments are sufficient to pay all the interest and to clear the mortgage debt by the end of the term of the mortgage.

Repayment Strategy

Relates to Interest Only mortgages where it is necessary to declare by what means the mortgage debt will be cleared when it comes to the end of the mortgage term. A lender may decline your application for a new mortgage if there is either no or an unsatisfactory repayment strategy.

Residential Property

In the context of mortgages, a Residential Property, is the property in which the mortgagor (the one borrowing the money) or the immediate family of the mortgagor resides and refer to as their home. It is not a Buy to Let, although a Buy to Let may be referred to as a Residential Buy to Let as opposed to a Commercial Buy to Let that would relate to a commercial or industrial property.

Right to Buy

A scheme that allows tenants in council houses to purchase their homes with a big discount.

Searches

Enquiries made by a purchaser or the purchaser's solicitor or conveyancer to places such as the Land Registry, the Land Charges Register and local authorities, to ensure there is nothing to cause concern about purchasing the intended property.

Secured

A loan or mortgage is said to be secured if the loan or the mortgage in question is linked to a property, such that, if the owner defaults on the monthly payments, the lender can force the sale of the property in order to recover its money.

Self Cert

A facility making mortgages available to those who cannot prove their level of income by the usual means such as supplying a copy of the previous months' payslips. The applicant for a mortgage merely needs to state the amount they earn. However, the lender needs to be able to demonstrate, if asked, the measures it took to satisfy itself that the mortgage was affordable. The availability of such mortgages has been severely restricted since the recession of 2008.

Seller

Also referred to as the Vendor, the Seller is the person or persons selling a property.

Settlement (Scotland)

The point at which the money is released to either purchase a property or remortgage an existing property and the transaction has completed. In England & Wales and Northern Ireland this is known as Completion.

Shared Ownership

A scheme to assist first-time buyers on to the housing ladder by allowing the occupier of a dwelling to buy a proportion of the property and pay rent on the remainder, typically to a local authority or housing association.

Sitting Tenant

A sitting tenant is one who entered into a tenancy before 1989 under the Rent Act 1977 and is regarded as a person who has security of tenure on the property. Such a tenant has the right to reside and a right to pay a 'fair rent' even if the property changed owners. Technically, any property bought with a tenant in residence becomes a sitting tenant, which is why one of the conditions in an offer of mortgage is that the property be sold with vacant possession. The rent was historically set by local housing officers and was usually somewhat below market value.

Staircasing

Staircasing relates to Shared Ownership and is the term used to describe purchasing an additional share of a property. The aim of Shared Ownership is to assist a person to get on the property ladder, which would otherwise be unaffordable and unattainable. As time goes on, maybe the owner has an increase in salary, perhaps due to a promotion at work and can now afford to buy a little bit more of the property. As time goes on, he repeats this and keeps on repeating it until he owns the entire property. This process of buying portions of the property is known as Staircasing.

Stamp Duty Land Tax

More commonly referred to as just Stamp Duty, it is a government tax levied on the purchase of land or property, to be paid by the purchaser at the time of making the purchase.

Standard Variable Rate (svr)

The Standard Variable Rate is a basic rate of interest that a lender wishes to charge for its mortgages. This rate of interest can be adjusted at any time, either up or down, at the discretion of the lender.

Stress Rate

The rate of percent that a lender requires the monthly rent to exceed the monthly mortgage payment in order to calculate the amount that it is prepared to lend on a Buy-to-Let.

Sub-Prime

Also known as non-conforming and non-status, Sub-Prime is a mortgage made available to those with a poor credit history, perhaps with, but not necessarily, County Court Judgements (CCJs) or for those who have been bankrupt or in arrears. Rates are likely to be higher than those available in the market as a whole and/or the Loan to Value may be restricted.

Subject to Contract

The terms of a transaction have been agreed provisionally but are not yet legally binding until all parties have signed and exchanged written contracts.

Tenancy Agreement

In terms of a typical residential property, this is usually (but not necessarily) an Assured Shorthold Tenancy Agreement (AST). It is a legal document setting out the conditions of a rental agreement between the landlord and a tenant, including the rights of both the tenant(s) and the landlord(s).

Tenants in Common

Whereas a property held as joint tenants are said to each own a 100% of the property, Tenants in Common is where owners each own a declared percentage of a property. There are advantages and disadvantages to holding a property as Tenants in Common and professional advice should be sought.

Term

The length of time over which your mortgage loan is to be repaid, typically 25 years.

Tied Broker

A mortgage adviser who sources mortgages from a panel of lenders rather than from the whole of the market.

Title

The legal right to ownership of a property.

Title Deeds

The documents showing the ownership of property.

Tracker Mortgage

Is a mortgage where the Standard Variable Rate (svr) and/or the initial incentive is defined as a fixed percentage above the Bank of England Base Rate. Therefore, if the Bank of England rate increases, the mortgage interest rate will also increase by the same amount. Similarly, if the Bank of England decreases its rate of interest, the mortgage interest rate will go down by the same amount. In other words, the prevailing interest rate on the mortgage is said to be tracking the Bank of England Base Rate.

Transfer Deeds

The legal document which transfers ownership of registered land.

Under Offer

If a property is said to be under offer, the seller has accepted an offer from a buyer. They have not yet exchanged contracts and so nothing is yet legally binding on either parties.

Unencumbered

A property is said to be unencumbered when it is not being used as security for any loan or mortgage. In other words, there is no mortgage or loan relating to or in any way associated with the property in question.

Valuation

In consideration of an application for a mortgage, the lender will wish to establish for itself the current market value of the property to which the application relates and will instruct an independent valuer/surveyor to provide a professional opinion of the value of the property. The cost of the valuation, the Valuation Fee, is usually borne by the mortgage applicant, whether it is a purchase or a remortgage and can sometimes be added to the mortgage as a way of financing that expense.

Vendor

An alternative word to seller. The person selling a property (or anything else for that matter) is known as the vendor.

Yield

Yield is used as a measure to determine the quality of an investment in property. It is calculated by dividing the annualised rent by the value of the property times 100.

Example:

Monthly Rent	=	910.00
Investment Value	=	195000.00
Monthly Rent x 12	=	10920.00 (Annualised Rent)
10920 / 195000	=	0.056
0.056 x 100	=	5.6
Therefore Yield	=	**5.6%**

ABOUT THE AUTHOR

Barry Mitchell entered the world of finance and became a 'Whole of Market' mortgage advisor in 1999. From 2002 to 2008 he was probably the most successful mortgage advisor in the United Kingdom and on one occasion, in 2006, was told by a lender that that month, he was the single largest provider of all their business. In 2004, he assisted the launch of a new mortgage brokerage which, within a year of commencing trading, became the 2nd largest mortgage brokerage in the country and all this whilst still running his own practice.

There are many facets to the man. He has been a professional salesman for over 40 years. He has run several businesses and for 15 years ran a specialist lining business, lining lakes, tanks and reservoirs as well as specialist flat roofing applications. He was a qualified electronics mechanic. He is passionate about gaining knowledge and using it for the benefit of others. He was licenced to practice as a hypno-therapist and psycho-analyst, although he never did practice – he just enjoyed studying the subject. He is a respected martial artist and still teaches his art all over the world. He cares about people and specialises in resolving their financial and business difficulties. It is this unique combination of being constantly driven by a thirst for knowledge, driven to improve the lives of others to help them become the best people they were ever destined to become, the unusual quality of being both technically minded and a 'people's person', that enables him, amongst other things, to take, dare we say, a boring subject like mortgages and explain their complexities in an enjoyable and interesting way and in a language that everybody can understand and even enjoy.

www.bmstrategist.co.uk

Made in the USA
Charleston, SC
14 May 2015